Healthy Me

STRESS LESS

Your Guide to Managing Stress

By Heather E. Schwartz

Consultant:
Jennifer F. Le, MD
Department of Psychiatry
Division of Child and Adolescent Psychiatry
University of Louisville School of Medicine

CAPSTONE PRESS
a capstone imprint

Snap Books are published by Capstone Press,
151 Good Counsel Drive, P.O. Box 669, Mankato, Minnesota 56002.
www.capstonepub.com

Books published by Capstone Press are manufactured with paper
containing at least 10 percent post-consumer waste.

Library of Congress Cataloging-in-Publication Data
Schwartz, Heather E.
  Stress less : your guide to managing stress / by Heather E. Schwartz.
     p. cm.—(Snap. Healthy me)
  Includes bibliographical references and index.
  Summary: "An introduction to stress including the causes of stress, its effects, and ways to handle worry,
anxiety, and stress"—Provided by publisher.
  ISBN 978-1-4296-6547-6 (library binding)
  ISBN 978-1-4296-7297-9 (paperback)
  1. Stress management—Juvenile literature. 2. Stress management for children—Juvenile literature.
I. Title. II. Series.
  RA785.S384 2012
  616.9'8—dc22
                                                                    2011008405

Editorial Credits:

Lori Shores, editor; Juliette Peters, designer; Svetlana Zhurkin, media researcher; Sarah Schuette, photo stylist;
    Marcy Morin, studio scheduler; Laura Manthe, production specialist

Photo Credits:

Capstone Studio: Karon Dubke, 5, 7, 10, 11, 12, 13, 15, 18, 21, 23, 26, 28, 29 (both); Dreamstime: Glenn Nagel, 9,
Ziprashantzi, cover (front); Getty Images: Gala Narezo, 17; iStockphoto: FineCollection, 20; Shutterstock: bioraven,
cover (middle right), dragon_fang, 19, Jessmine, cover (top left), John Barry de Nicola, 25, muzsy, 14, Quang Ho,
cover (bottom left), takayuki, 24

Essential content terms are **bold** and are defined at the bottom of the page where they first appear.

Printed in the United States of America in North Mankato, Minnesota.
032011   006110CGF11

Table of Contents

Chapter 1

Day In, Day Out

School Daze

Buzz! Buzz! Without opening your eyes, you switch off your alarm and drift back to sleep. Half an hour later, you jolt awake. Oh, no—running late again! After a quick shower, you gulp down breakfast and race to catch the bus.

By the time you get to school, you've caught your breath enough to chat with friends. All too soon, the bell rings, and the real pressure is on. First there's a pop quiz in history. Next you're called on to answer a tough question in math. In language arts, you give an oral report. Later you'll have to prove yourself in gym. Plus you have a music lesson. The teacher is sure to notice you haven't practiced!

As you rush from subject to subject, you struggle with other social **stressors**. Who will be your partner for the big science project? Who will you sit with at lunch today?

stressor: a situation that causes stress

Life Goes On

You'd like to relax a little after school. But on Mondays and Wednesdays, you have tennis practice. After-school clubs meet on Tuesdays and Thursdays. On Friday afternoons you do odd jobs to earn your allowance. The weekends are always packed too. You love everything you do. But you barely have time for other activities, such as playing with your dog or spending time with friends.

At dinner, your parents ask about your day. They're probably just being friendly, but do they really have to ask about your homework? You'll get to it! Once your homework is done, you have to get your school bag and clothes ready for the next day. Then you might get a chance to watch TV and have a snack. After the show, it's lights-out. You collapse into bed, but your mind is racing. You can't fall asleep. That's **stress**!

stress: mental, emotional, or physical strain

Healthy Tip

Caffeine in chocolate, soda, tea, and energy drinks can keep you awake. If you drink only decaffeinated drinks after 4 p.m., you'll have an easier time falling asleep at bedtime.

What Stress?

Lots of situations can cause stress. In a nationwide poll, 875 kids aged 9 to 13 listed their most common stressors. Here are the top three.

36% grades, school, and homework

21% friends, teasing, and gossip

32% family issues

Chapter 2

Aaarhhh!

What Exactly Is Stress?

Stress is a feeling you get when you're under pressure. It's a mental state. It can also cause physical symptoms such as stomachaches and headaches.

When you feel stressed, your body releases **hormones**. Your heart rate increases, and you breathe faster. Your body gets ready to react quickly by fighting or running away. This "fight or flight" response can help with some stressors. For example, if an animal is about to attack you, fighting and running are good solutions.

Most likely, you face other kinds of stressors. Suppose a teacher wrongly accuses you of cheating. Or maybe a coach embarrasses you during practice. Your body may tell you to fight or run, but neither will help. You'll be able to work things out if you stay calm. That's one reason managing stress is important.

hormone: a chemical made by the body

If you're feeling stressed, focus on your breathing. Pay attention to each inhale and exhale. Slowing your breathing will help you relax. To do this, count to three as you inhale and again as you exhale.

What Causes Stress?

Stress is a normal reaction when things aren't going your way. You may feel stressed if you're running late or if you don't know an answer in class. But stress can strike when life is great too. Suppose you've just landed the lead in the school play. Sure, you're happy. But whenever there's a change in your life, you have to adjust. Until you do, you may feel stressed.

Even everyday activities that are usually fun may start to feel stressful. Stress can be a signal that something about a situation has changed. Maybe your two best friends are fighting. Or maybe your schedule has gotten so packed, you have no time for yourself.

Healthy Tip

You can't control every situation, but you can always stay hopeful that things will work out. Wearing a loose rubber band on your wrist can help. Snap it gently to remind yourself to think positively.

Stress From Within

Stress doesn't always come from **external** situations, like a crabby coach or trouble with a teacher. Sometimes it comes from within. Do you put a lot of pressure on yourself to make straight As? Do you try to fit in with a certain crowd? Trying your best is always good. But it's important to remember that no one succeeds at everything all the time. It's OK to make mistakes. It's OK to rethink your goals.

external: outside your body or mind

When kids put too much pressure on themselves, they often feel overwhelmed. That feeling can lead to poor decisions. They might decide there's no point in studying. They might turn to more extreme measures, such as taking drugs, drinking alcohol, or hurting themselves. Some kids even consider suicide. But these measures are never the answer. No problem is ever worth hurting yourself or others.

You can deal with any problem. You just need the right solution. Sometimes finding the solution takes a team effort. Even the most difficult problems can be handled with help from your family and friends.

Healthy Tip

Talk to friends, parents, teachers, or other trusted adults about your problems. Sharing your thoughts and feelings can relieve stress. Plus, they may be able to see your problems differently and suggest possible solutions.

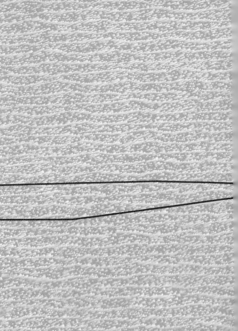

Good Stress vs. Bad Stress

While stress can be difficult to manage, sometimes it's actually helpful. When you feel stressed before a big test, you're motivated to study harder. The physical energy created by stress can be used to help you win a soccer game. Stress can also signal that it's time to make a change. For example, it may help you realize you want to quit a club you don't enjoy. But good stress becomes bad stress when it sticks around too long.

Chronic stress develops in situations that aren't fixed quickly. For example, it could develop if you're stuck in a class that's too difficult. It could develop if you're the victim of ongoing bullying.

Chronic stress can lead to emotional problems, such as depression and **anxiety**. It may help to talk to a parent, counselor, therapist, or other health care professional. With help, your stress can be reduced or relieved. It may not happen overnight, but working together, you'll be able to find ways to cope.

Healthy Tip

You can relieve stress by taking control. Brainstorm ideas about how to change your stressful situation. Then put your plans into action or talk to someone who can help.

chronic: long lasting or recurring
anxiety: a feeling of worry or fear

Chapter 3

Am I Stressed?

Stress can cause physical, mental, and emotional symptoms. They're different for everyone. That difference can make it tough to tell whether you're stressed at all.

What Does Stress Feel Like?

Stress can affect your physical, mental, and emotional well-being. Some people get angry when they're stressed. Others feel sad. You might feel frustrated, overwhelmed, or even afraid. These feelings may come up right when something happens. You might feel angry when you hear your parents or friends argue. But stress can also trigger these feelings when nothing unusual is happening. For instance, maybe you feel on edge because you think an argument might happen.

Feelings brought on by stress can change how you act. You might have trouble concentrating in class. You may eat more or less than you normally do. Or you may be cranky toward your family and friends. If you catch yourself behaving differently, ask yourself—"Am I stressed?"

Stress Gets Physical

It's bad enough that stress can cause unpleasant feelings. But stress can also cause physical problems. Do you feel achy when you work on math homework? Are you sick to your stomach before tennis matches? Sure, you could be coming down with the flu. But if you notice a pattern, it's possible your symptoms are stress-related.

It might be tempting to shrug off headaches, hives, and other symptoms of stress. But they shouldn't be ignored. Symptoms are signs that you need to reduce your stress. Chronic stress can eventually weaken the **immune system**. That means if you don't manage your stress, you'll be more likely to get sick. If you're having physical symptoms of stress, tell your parents, and ask to see a doctor for help.

immune system: the part of the body that protects against germs and disease

Just the Facts

A national survey by the American Psychological Association found 30 percent of middle school kids get headaches from stress.

18

Stress Hurts

The physical symptoms of stress can be surprising.
These are some of the more common symptoms.

dizziness

headaches

grinding teeth

aching back,
neck,
shoulders

dry mouth

heartburn

change in appetite

upset stomach

increased
sweating

shaky legs

hives

Stress and You

Some people feel stressed by events other people love, such as going to parties. When others don't feel the same way, they might tell you to just get over it. That's not always easy. In fact, that kind of advice can make you even more stressed.

It doesn't really matter if other people have an easier time with things that stress you out. The only thing that matters is how you feel. Remember, your feelings are **valid** whether you're stressing about a party or moving to a new town.

You don't have to let stress rule your life, though. You can overcome it. If you're worried about a party, you could go with a friend. If you're moving to a new town, you might think of ways to introduce yourself and start conversations.

valid: acceptable

Rate Your Stress

On a scale of 1-10, rate the stress you'd expect to feel in specific situations:

giving a speech in class

trying to score in a game

moving to a new town

having a conflict with a friend

talking to a teacher about a poor grade

going to a party alone

starting a new school

Now look back over your ratings and total them up. The lower your score, the less you worry about things ahead of time. If you scored high, you have a lot of stress. Think about ways to handle these situations.

Healthy Tip

When you get enough sleep, you can handle stress better. Kids need nine to 10 hours of sleep each night to feel rested. Getting enough downtime during the day can also help you manage stress.

Chapter 4

Managing Stress

Stress is a fact of life. You can't always avoid it, but there are positive ways to deal with it.

Get Organized

Are you often late for school because you can't find your homework? Do you forget to bring home books you need? Have you ever left a major project until the last minute? If you answered yes to any of these questions, you know how stressful school can be. Even if you're not a planner by nature, getting organized can help.

If remembering assignments causes you stress, try keeping track in a notebook or planner. Write down assignments throughout the day, and read your notes later. Some kids do homework in the same place and at the same time each day. Packing up finished homework in your book bag right away can also help. That way, there's no chance it'll get lost before the next morning.

When you feel overwhelmed by a long-term project, it's tempting to put it off. But you can avoid that last-minute stress if you chip away at it slowly. The first day it's assigned, you can get off to a good start by setting up a plan. The same approach works for upcoming tests. If you start early, you'll have time to study or get extra help. That way, there's no need to stress about failing the assignment or the class.

Healthy Tip

Keep a calendar that lists your tests and project due dates as well as after-school activities. Take time to look ahead each week, so you can plan for whatever is coming up.

Cut Back

Is your schedule so packed that it feels like you barely have time to breathe? Your time and energy are limited resources. You can't say yes to everything. Homework has to get done, of course. But you may be able to cut back on other activities.

Think about which activities you truly enjoy and create a new schedule. Make sure it also includes some real downtime. Then you can relax, recharge, and give your all to the activities you love.

Cutting back may seem impossible at first. What would your dad say if you quit softball? How would your friends feel if you stopped taking horseback riding lessons with them? How can you give up your weekend volunteer work at the animal shelter? The animals need you so much!

Saying no isn't easy, but remember, you don't have to do everything at once. Maybe next year you'll have more time for softball. For now, you can play pickup games and practice with your dad. Maybe you could do some activities once a month instead of every week.

Just the Facts

Studies show 77 percent of kids wish they had more free time.

Big Problems

Some problems are bigger than busy schedules and bad grades. Maybe a family member is sick or struggling with drugs or alcohol. Maybe your parents argue a lot. If your family is having trouble, don't be afraid to talk to someone outside your family. Teachers, guidance counselors, and youth group leaders can help you find information and support groups. Spending time at a friend's house when home life is stressful can also help.

Peers can cause big problems too. Maybe you're bothered by gossip or feel threatened by bullies. In some cases, you may be able to ignore the situation. You could avoid reading mean texts and online posts.

If you're really upset or scared, however, you'll need some support. Trying to handle everything yourself only adds more stress to an already stressful situation. Can your parents drive you to school? Would they consider getting you a cell phone? Friends might be willing to walk with you to classes. Teachers might also have ideas that can help during the school day. If you're worried you'll sound like a tattletale, remember it's never tattling if you are sticking up for yourself.

peer: a person of the same age as another

Just the Facts

A recent study showed that 42 percent of students in grades four through eight had experienced online bullying.

Healthy Tip

Taking a walk can help relieve stress. When you exercise, your body makes hormones that can reduce physical symptoms of stress and also help to improve your mood.

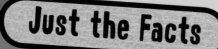

Keep Stress in Check

Sometimes stress can sneak up on you. You're not even aware that it's building when—wham! Stress strikes, and it doesn't feel good.

What's the best way to prevent that from happening? Stay strong. That doesn't mean you have to build big muscles. You could try something that's healthy for you. Maybe you want to eat more fruits and vegetables and fewer sugary snacks. Or you might focus on getting plenty of sleep at night. Building up your self-confidence is another way to stay strong. You could try thinking more positively and worrying less.

When you do feel stressed, you now have plenty of ideas you can use to make yourself feel better. Some fixes might be quick. Others might take longer. But you'll get through the situation, no matter how big or small. With your new skills, you'll be ready to handle anything.

Conquer Your Stress

People relieve stress in many different ways.
Here are some healthy suggestions.

If you're by yourself:

- play with a pet
- listen to music
- write in a journal
- take a warm shower
- read a book
- take a short nap

If you feel like being around others:

- play sports with friends
- talk to a friend, sibling, or parent
- watch a cheerful movie with a buddy

If you're in the mood for exercise:

- take a walk
- practice a sport
- go swimming
- go for a bike ride

Glossary

anxiety (ang-ZYE-uh-tee)—a feeling of worry or fear

chronic (KRON-ik)—long lasting or recurring

depression (di-PRE-shuhn)—an emotional disorder that causes people to feel sad and tired

external (ek-STUR-nuhl)—on the outside

hormone (HOR-mohn)—a chemical made by a gland in the body that affects a person's growth and development

immune system (i-MYOON SISS-tuhm)—the part of the body that protects against germs and diseases

peer (PIHR)—a person of the same age as another

stress (STRESS)—mental, emotional, or physical strain

stressor (STRESS-uhr)—a situation that creates stress

valid (VAL-id)—acceptable

Read More

Biegel, Gina M. *The Stress Reduction Workbook for Teens: Mindfulness Skills to Help You Deal with Stress.* Oakland, Calif.: Instant Help Books, 2009.

Burstein, John. *Past Tense: Healthy Ways to Manage Stress.* Slim Goodbody's Life Skills 101. New York: Crabtree Pub., 2011.

Harmon, Daniel E. *Frequently Asked Questions about Overscheduling and Stress.* FAQ: Teen Life. New York: Rosen Pub., 2010.

Internet Sites

FactHound offers a safe, fun way to find Internet sites related to this book. All of the sites on FactHound have been researched by our staff.

Here's all you do:

Visit *www.facthound.com*

Type in this code: 9781429665476

Super-cool stuff! Check out projects, games and lots more at **www.capstonekids.com**

Index